C000057705

ANIMAL ATTACKS

Compiled by Lars Ryan

&

Edited by Tom Lyons

ANIMAL ATTACKS

Copyright © 2020 Lars Ryan & Tom
Lyons

All rights reserved. No part of this may
be reproduced in any form or by any
means without the prior consent of the
author, except for brief quotes used in
reviews.

All information and opinions expressed
in *Animal Attacks* are based upon
personal perspectives and experiences of
those who were generous enough to
submit them. The creator does not
purport the information presented in
this book is based on any accurate,
current, or valid scientific knowledge.

Acknowledgments

It's certainly no easy task for people to discuss their encounters with ferocious animals. I'd like to personally thank the many good people out there who took the time and energy to put their experiences into writing.

Out of respect for those who were involved, a few of the names have been altered or replaced with "anonymous".

Would you like to see your report in an issue of *"Animal Attacks"*?

If so, all you have to do is type up a summary of your experience, and email it to Lars at:

When.Animals.Bite@gmail.com

Special Offer

If you submit a report and it is accepted, you will receive an exclusive paperback copy signed by Lars, shortly after the book is released. If you'd like to participate in that offer, be sure to include your mailing address in the email.

WARNING

Some of the following stories might be
considered too intense for children.
Parental discretion is advised.

Contents

Introduction

Hello, all. My name is Lars Ryan, and I got the idea to put this book together while dealing with the trauma from my violent encounter with a wild animal. Due to an out-of-court settlement, I'm unable to reveal any details about the facility or the organization that was responsible for looking after the animal. That's also why I am publishing this book under an alias; I want to be extra cautious. Therefore, no, 'Lars' is not my real name. However, I still wanted to find a way to share my experience with others.

While undergoing nearly a year of psychological therapy, my counselor granted me a series of tips, many of which were quite useful. One thing he suggested I did was to visit various forums on the web and attempt to connect with others who have faced frightening confrontations with animals. At first, I was skeptical about the idea, but I quickly felt the relief from the exchange of stories. It felt great to speak to people who knew that level of fear. When animals attack, it so suddenly feels as if you're a mere caveman trying to defend yourself from an ambush. One aspect that I've noticed nearly everyone agrees on—we sure did underestimate the strength of our aggressors. I know so many TV shows, documentaries, and books mention that, but I don't believe you can appreciate it fully until you've experienced it firsthand. It's remarkable how vulnerable it can make humans feel. Pound for pound, people can't even compare.

You might not be surprised to learn that we're never informed about a large portion of the animal attacks that occur around the world every year. With politics, celebrity gossip, sports, and technology occupying the top news stories, there is little room left for these awkward and terrifying encounters. Make no mistake; many of them are reported to the media but never redistributed to the public eye. As soon as I realized that, I remember wishing that there was an efficient way to get these stories out there. I truly believe that not only does it bring awareness to how unpredictable animals can be, but it serves as therapy for survivors who might have PTSD.

I want to make it very clear that the intention of creating this book is not to portray animals as monsters. When animals become aggressive with us, it is almost always because we have made them feel threatened, and to be rather honest, I think they have every reason not to trust our species; all you have to do is consider the amount of destruction we've done to nature. I can't blame the animals one bit. And in no way would I wish revenge on the animal that attacked me; that's not at all my style.

Less than a year ago, I came across one of Tom Lyon's book series' that contains a similar format but has nothing to do with the subject matter. I enjoyed the reading format of the series and decided I would replicate it with a topic that I had had experience with. As I had suspected, the act of compiling and editing these recounts was very therapeutic for my brain, and I can't emphasize enough how grateful I am to everyone who submitted. I know there will likely be some people who will read this book purely for entertainment, and that is okay, but please be respectful of anyone who was willing to reveal their true identity.

I hope you enjoy the read,

-Lars

Report #1

As I stated in the introduction, I'm not going to reveal the location of where my incident took place. Honestly, I don't even feel comfortable reviewing the region. I want to retain complete privacy on the matter. As with so many other animal attacks, none of the media outlets mentioned it or even knew about it. Nonetheless, I hope you find my story intriguing.

It all started when a close friend of mine invited me to a big cat rescue facility on a beautiful late spring day. My friend, who I will give the alias of Joseph, was a very confident and trustworthy sort of guy; therefore, I didn't even put much thought into whether this would be a safe adventure. Joseph happened to be dating a woman who worked at this facility, and he wanted me to meet her for quite some time, but I had always been busy when they were available. So, I took the opportunity to not only meet my friend's new girlfriend but also to take part in an activity I had never done before. Unfortunately, I would end up regretting that decision.

Perhaps the trauma has somehow tricked me into believing this detail was more prominent than it actually was, but I did have an off-putting feeling right as Joseph and I pulled into the parking lot.

It was almost like my instincts were
warning me that I shouldn't be there,
that I should head on home or at least
remain in that parking lot while my
friend did his thing. But I've never really
been the type to back out of things once
I agreed to participate, and it felt as
though that would be the rude thing to
do. So, I did my best to disregard the
feeling and continued toward the facility
entrance. When I told someone else
about that worrisome feeling, they
claimed that our instincts are extremely
powerful and that the feeling likely came
from the fact that I was nearing large
predators. I've read up on that idea and
found several other similar opinions;
perhaps there is something to that
notion.

Anyway, when we entered the
facility, Joseph's girlfriend, who I'll give

the alias of 'Megan', was there to greet
up. She was a taller, athletically built
individual; clearly, she did a great job of
taking care of her health, and I didn't
doubt that she did the same with the
animals that she was hired to look after.
I came to learn we had come during off-
hours, so there was only one other
individual there in addition to the three
of us. He was another employee, and I'll
give him the name 'Charlie'. Charlie's
primary duty was to manage the place,
and it was he who ultimately gave the
okay for Megan to invite us over there
for a private visit.

After a bit of chitchat, the first
thing we did was head on over to the
bobcat pen. The creature quickly
amazed me; it was the first time I had
ever seen one in the flesh. Its fur was so
beautiful, and I remember thinking its

paws were enormous in ratio to its body. We got to watch as Megan went inside the pen and laid out some food for the magnificent creature. It impressed me how she didn't seem at all worried when stepping into its domain; I imagine you get pretty used to that after working there for as long as she had. Next, we saw a large bird; I want to say it was a condor or something like that. Whatever it was, it was huge.

Eventually, we made our way to the cougar pen. Megan explained that the facility cared for this cougar since it was a cub. She told us a story about how its mother was poached. It was terribly sad. Luckily, they were able to rescue three of the four cubs; they were found soon before they could've starved to death. The animal that Megan had cared for was a female, and she claimed that it was one of the gentlest animals she had ever interacted with. She was so confident with this creature that she volunteered to let Joseph and I into the enclosure.

I was a little bit nervous as I stepped into the enclosure, but seeing how affectionate the creature was toward Megan quickly helped my nerves to relax. The cougar slowly strolled from one person to the next, lightly brushing itself against our legs, much like what the typical house cat would do. This trend continued for a few minutes while Joseph and I bombarded Megan with questions about the fascinating animal. I remember it so vividly; ironically, she was talking about their hunting habits as I felt the weight against my back, along with what seemed like a series of knives piercing my skin. I instantly fell to my knees—which I believe is what ultimately saved me because the cougar also lost its balance. Its teeth did nick the rear of my neck, but it didn't manage to get a firm grip. As I desperately tried to rise to my feet and separate myself from the animal's reach, I could feel its jaws latch onto the outside of my left hip, but my adrenaline was pumping so hard by that point that it wasn't even all that painful.

While all of this was happening, Joseph and Megan's voices seemed like faraway echoes as they shouted at the cougar, attempting to pull it away from its target. I'll never forget the strength of that creature. It was as if it went from acting like an oversized pet to a ferocious killing machine within the blink of an eye. Of course, there was nothing I could think of that would've provoked the animal. Somehow, I had to have spooked it or it decided that I was the weakest of the humans, thus triggering predatory instincts.

Even though it felt like an eternity to me, Joseph and Megan said the struggle only lasted less than thirty seconds. Unfortunately, Megan had to smack the cougar a few times with a nearby tool, but if she hadn't, there's a damn good chance it would've returned to my throat. If that had happened, my windpipes more than likely would've gotten crushed, and I would've died. As the couple helped me to my feet, I saw the animal on the other side of the enclosure. I was very dizzy at the time, but I remember thinking that the cat looked so different compared to when we first entered through the gate. The only way I know how to describe what

I'm talking about is that its eyes had a predatory gaze.

A wave of confusion swept over me as they helped me through the exit. Even though I was very perturbed, I also remember experiencing an overwhelming sense of gratitude for still being alive. You hear about that sort of thing happening all the time to people who got so close to death. Quite honestly, I think I've cherished life far more than I did before the event; when considering that, I'm almost glad the powerful animal attacked me.

I was in such an intense state of shock that I hadn't even noticed the chunk of meat that had been taken out of my leg until we were waiting for the ambulance. It was only as I looked at it that I began to feel the immense pain; it's interesting how things can work that way. Both Megan and Charlie were extremely caring and helpful as we awaited the paramedics, and they even came to visit me in the emergency room. Much of that day is like a dream; everything that happened after the attack is rather hazy. And when they put me on morphine as a means to help suppress the pain, my memory of the rest of that day became even vaguer.

For the sake of making a long, boring part short, I had crappy health insurance at the time, and the medical bills got me into a ton of debt. I ended up settling out of court with the animal care facility, and they worked something out to cover everything I owed. Frankly, the idea that I was going to have to pay off that enormous bill was scarier than the cougar attack, itself. The owners and employees of the facility seemed very worried that I was going to make a big deal of the whole thing and gain them a ton of negative publicity. Luckily for them, I'm not the type of guy to make a big fuss. And since I respect everyone who was involved, I certainly didn't want to taint anyone's reputation. They were trying to do something memorable; it was merely an accident. Also, it's not as if anyone forced me inside the pen. I was more than aware that there was risk associated with that, regardless of how Megan acted.

I graciously accepted the offer and signed a bunch of papers, stating that I would never mention the facility or the names of anyone affiliated with it. I don't know too many of the details, but I bet it wasn't easy to avoid the press on the matter when you consider the small number of ears that heard about what had happened. It makes you wonder what many people must go through, daily, to ensure that certain things don't get exposed to the public.

There has been quite a bit of work done on my leg throughout the years, and I have to admit that it looks way closer to normal than I ever would've imagined. I remember almost fainting from how mutilated it looked when I saw the entire wound for the first time. I had to force myself to close my eyes and focus on something else.

Well, that about does it for my experience. I hope you enjoy the following reports.

-Lars

Report #2

Year: 1998

Location: Carmel, CA

Hey there, my name is William, and I endured a traumatic experience when I was at the age of 17. Truly, it's something I wish I could erase from my memory, for so many reasons.

My parents were going through a bit of a rough patch; they needed some time to work things out, so I had been staying at my grandma's place, which was only a few miles away. My grandma and I were close, so it started as a good strategy to relieve my mind from everything that was going on between my mom and dad. My black lab, Pablo, came to stay with me at my grandma's place. He and I were very close; my parents gave him to me as a birthday present when I turned 11.

My grandma lived in a picturesque part of town; it was on a hill and looked out onto beautiful forestland. I can remember appreciating the feeling when I was there, something that is often under looked by moody teenagers. Without a doubt, Pablo loved it too.

Anyway, it was a weekend night, and I had been out to the movies with this girl that I had a huge crush on. The date went well, so I was in a good mood when I walked in through the door of my grandma's home. I thought it was odd that many of the lights were still on; she was usually the type to be in bed and watching TV by 10 o'clock. It was past midnight. Next, I noticed that Pablo hadn't run to the door to greet me like he always did. That immediately triggered a knot in my stomach.

"Pablo!?" I heard my grandma's voice call out from somewhere outside the house. I rushed into the living room and spotted her on the balcony. As I neared the door, I heard eerie yips coming from somewhere in the distance.

"Grandma, what's going on?" I said, "Where's Pablo?"

My voice startled her, and she jumped before turning to face me. I could see tears in her eyes; they were tears of worry. I didn't even need to receive an explanation before I ran inside, grabbed a flashlight from the pantry, and sprinted back out into the night. The terrain became harder to maneuver, the closer I got to the commotion. The noises were so eerie; it felt as though I was running directly toward a pack of hyenas.

The first thing I saw was the glow from several pairs of eyes as the flashlight landed upon them. That spooked the pack of coyotes enough to prompt them to back off from what they had gathered around. It's incredibly challenging for me to write this, as the feelings of devastation quickly return. If it hadn't been for Pablo's blue collar wrapped around the neck area of the skeleton, I probably would've insisted that it wasn't him. There was hardly any meat left, and a couple of limbs had already been severed and taken somewhere else. As I kneeled in front of the mess, I felt teeth sink into my upper left arm near my elbow. Without hesitating, I swung the flashlight against the coyote's head and bashed it repeatedly until it finally released its clench. But I was as I began to rise to my feet that another coyote latched onto my right forearm, causing me to drop the flashlight. I used my injured left arm to hit the second coyote in the face, which had little effect. Out of desperation, I then gouged my thumb into its left eye socket. Soon, the animal squealed from the irritation and stepped away from me.

Recognizing that that was my chance to get away, I picked up the flashlight and dashed up the hill toward the house, assuming it would be any moment until I felt the pack catch up to me and take another bite.

"Get inside, Grandma!" I yelled as soon as I spotted her on the balcony. She did as I instructed, and we closed the door behind us.

I lost all stamina at that moment; I dropped to the floor and began balling my eyes out. I couldn't believe I had lost Pablo like that, completely out of nowhere. When I told Grandma about what I had found, she repeatedly apologized, stating that she never would've let my dog outside if she knew those coyotes were in the area. I couldn't blame her; I would've done the same. I always let Pablo out to run around on his own when we were still living at my parents' house. Quite honestly, I never thought coyotes were much of a threat to dogs of that size. Neither did anyone I knew. I've never been one to yearn for the death of an animal, but I felt such rage toward that pack of coyotes that I had them all exterminated. Since they had attacked a human, it didn't take too much convincing, and my grandma was happy to have them off the property; the idea of having aggressive animals like that in her yard terrified her.

A few days later, we had a burial for Pablo, which my parents attended. They were devastated, as they also loved that dog with all their hearts. I think the tragedy brought us all closer together, as it reminded us that we must not take the things we love for granted; that was the silver lining.

I sometimes still have trouble accepting that that whole thing happened; it seemed like a scene from a nightmare, rather than real life. I'm sure most people will chuckle at the idea of coyotes being dangerous to humans or even large dogs, but I warn you not to underestimate them. It's amazing what even the smallest of critters are capable of when they work together as a team.

-Submitted by William G.

Report #3

I had a very frightening experience while I was on my honeymoon in Kauai. I'm sorry to say I've been afraid to go back into the ocean ever since.

My wife and I had been drinking mojitos on the beach in the early afternoon when I decided to go for a swim. We were at the beach outside of our hotel, and each time we had gone swimming before that, it had been a very pleasant experience; therefore, I felt no reason to have my guard up. We swam out to water that was probably only six to seven feet deep. It was crystal clear, so I could see most of everything that was around me. Suddenly, I noticed a dorsal fin protrude above the surface about ten feet away from my location. For obvious reasons, I got pretty nervous but was relieved when I confirmed it was a dolphin.

"Honey, there are dolphins over here!" I excitedly shouted to my wife, who was probably about fifteen feet closer to the shore. We had seen a bunch of interesting sea life since we had been on the island, but my wife kept saying how she wished for us to see dolphins. As she happily swam toward me, two more dolphins playfully swam underneath my feet. When one of them circled and neared me at the surface, I was able to extend my hand and pet it. It started as one of the coolest experiences; it felt like a fantasy in paradise. I believe it was that same dolphin that soon turned around and headed back toward me.

Soon after I once again extended my hand to pet the aquatic creature, I felt the rough tugging sensation. It was before the pain even had a chance to set in that I saw the red tint in the water in front of me. My wife began to scream as I lifted my arm above the water to get a better look; my hand was missing. I stared at it in horror as blood spirted from the severed limb. I don't know if it was because I was in shock, but I couldn't believe how hard it was to paddle without my right hand. I should also mention that I am right-handed, so the motion of swimming felt awkward in general. I remember it so vividly as the two lifeguards were already on their way into the water, and one of them was shouting for me to stop swimming. I'd later find out it was for two reasons. One of them was that flailing my arms would increase the blood flow, thus causing me to lose blood at a faster rate; the other reason was that they assumed a shark had attacked me, and the splashing could trigger an additional predatory response.

The lifeguards helped me out of the water with ease, and it was only a few minutes before I was in an ambulance on my way to the hospital. It's amazing how quickly a beautiful experience can go dark. It felt like it happened in a mere split second. We're led to believe that dolphins don't bite people; thus, I was reckless when they approached me. Now I'm forced to live with a hook for a hand because I wasn't better educated on the risks.

On the bright side of things, the resort paid me a gigantic settlement, and I haven't had to worry about working another day since. The catch was that I wasn't allowed to speak of where exactly my accident happened because the owners had convinced themselves they'd lose a ton of business on account that nobody would want to swim near their beach anymore.

My wife ended up leaving me a few years later and took half of that payout. Of course, I have no way of knowing for sure whether or not it was the reason, but I felt she looked at me differently right after my hand was bitten off. There were a few occasions where she was in a really bad mood, and when I tried to comfort her, she yelled at me to not touch her with my hook. She would always then apologize and explain how she didn't mean it like that, but it was obvious she was turned off by the whole thing.

I do believe that my accident was a very freak thing and that the chances are incredibly slim; still, be careful if you ever have the opportunity to swim with dolphins. Yes, they're highly intelligent creatures, but just like us, they can be moody and unpredictable.

-Submitted by anonymous

Report #4

Hi, my name is Nicole, and I endured a very scary situation after being coaxed by my ex-boyfriend to hold one of his exotic pets. Never will I be pressured to do anything like it again.

I grew up in a small town in New Mexico known as Raton, and to be honest, there's not a whole lot to do there; therefore, I suppose it's the ideal place for young men to invest in dangerous pets. I was 20 years old when this incident happened, and my ex-boyfriend was 21. He went through this phase where he was really into making homemade margaritas, and we had already had a couple when he decided to bring out his pet centipede that he named Taz. It was a weird as hell name for a giant bug, and I don't think he even knew if it was a male or female. To say that that creature was hideous would be an understatement; I remember having to watch it eat a mouse once, and I wanted to barf.

Anyway, we were a little liquored up when my ex started talking about how I should face my fears and hold Taz. For whatever reason, I gave in, and before I knew it, I was holding the strange creature. The sensation of its like a million legs crawling up and down my forearm was chilling, and at the same time, tickled. I distinctly remember how I was about to admit that the creature was sort of cute when suddenly, I felt the most agonizing sting. I immediately saw the puncture marks, as the fangs (or whatever they are) on giant centipedes are huge. I immediately swung my arm, causing the foul creature to fly off me and land on the couch. It quickly crawled off the couch and went underneath some other furniture before my ex could catch it.

As I was washing the wound with cold water, I began to feel very nauseous and dizzy. My ex asked me if I was okay because I guess I was also slurring my words. Even though he was drunk, he demanded that I get into the car so that he could drive me to the hospital. He was worried that I had had an intense allergic reaction to the centipede's venom and that I needed medical attention right away. I'm glad he convinced me to go to the ER because it turned out my body was undergoing a reaction that was more severe than normal. Since we arrived at the hospital before the symptoms could escalate, I ended up only being there for a few hours.

A few days later, my ex was also bitten by the centipede for the first time when he finally located it running across his living room floor. Luckily, his body didn't react the same way to the venom. It wasn't much longer before he got rid of the thing. I'm pretty sure he drove out to the desert and set if free.

I can't say I'll ever understand why he had that thing for a pet, but I suppose boys will be boys. One thing is for sure—I'll never go near one of them again.

-Submitted by Nicole A.

Report #5

My name is Mark, and I had a scary experience with a freshwater fish while vacationing with my parents in the Northwoods of Wisconsin. This incident happened 12 years ago when I was 19 years of age.

While my father was growing up, his family would take an annual trip to a lake house in Eagle River, Wisconsin. Some of his favorite memories involve those trips, so he decided to carry on the tradition with his kids.

The beautiful summer day had started normally; we spent the late morning hours tubing and waterskiing. My sister and I decided to have a little competition of who could stay up the longest on a single ski. She went first and wasn't able to stay up very long at all. When I went next, I ended up crushing her record with ease. I remember how it was as I was waiting for my dad to circle the boat around to pick me up, I started to get a strange feeling; something felt wrong, but I couldn't put my finger on what it was. It had never bothered me too much before, but the notion that the water was too dark to see what was around me suddenly became very disconcerting.

The boat had almost made its way over to me when it happened; searing pain began to radiate from the front of my foot, mainly around the area of my big toe. It felt like something with immense strength was viciously tugging on me. I started splashing around profusely, fighting to pull my limb away from whatever the hell had grabbed it. I was so close to the boat that my sister yanked on my lifejacket, attempting to pull me up and into the boat. My dad soon noticed the struggle and ran over to assist. At that moment, I remember thinking that a bull shark had attacked me. I knew that they were able to survive in freshwater, and I thought that somehow one had managed to make its way into our lake. I was so sure that's what it was because it felt so damn powerful.

It was as my dad and sister helped pull me into the boat that they saw the culprit—a large muskellunge, also known as 'musky'. Since I was turned toward the boat as they helped me in, I didn't even get a glimpse of it. According to them, it was as my foot made it to the surface that the fish let go and swam back down into the depths. I almost fainted as I lay on the floor of the speedboat; the sight of my missing big toe was a lot to bear.

For those of you who don't know, the musky is the largest fish in the pike family, and although quite rare, it's native to North America. If you've never seen what they look like, they look a lot like barracudas. Their teeth are extremely sharp and can easily tear through human flesh. The largest one caught on record came in at 65 pounds. I have no way of knowing the size of the one that attacked me, but let me tell you, it felt very heavy. Musky attacks are incredibly rare, but they do happen from time to time; I certainly wasn't the first to find myself in that frightening situation.

Fortunately, my dad found a basic first aid kit somewhere in the boat and rushed to bandage the wound. My sister was saying everything she could to make things seem less scary, but I could tell she was extremely nervous. I had never endured a wound that dramatic before then, so I had no way of knowing if the amount of blood loss could be fatal. I at least knew that it was critical to remain as calm as possible after facing an injury like that, so that's what I tried to focus.

When we arrived back to shore, we all piled into the car and drove straight to the hospital. They immediately gave me something that helped me to cope with the pain and calm my nerves. I can remember this one younger male nurse talking about how he had heard of a very similar incident once before. There was no chance of getting my toe back; otherwise they might've been able to reattach it since we had gotten to the hospital right away.

I've been missing part of my foot ever since, but as time passes, you're able to get used to anything. Still, I don't think I'll ever swim in a lake or large river ever again. It's impossible to know what is lurking around you.

-Submitted by Mark T.

Report #6

The following incident happened in Sarasota over a decade ago. I feel I should warn the readers that it might be too gruesome for some.

My name is Vill, and when my family moved from Russia to Florida back when I was in my teenage years, I used to do a bit of babysitting so that I'd have some spending money. I've always liked children, so the job was a very good fit for me. A man and woman that lived down the street from me would go out almost every weekend night, so they would constantly ask me to babysit for them. They had the cutest children—one girl was at the age of seven, and the younger one was three. I had worked for this family probably around 15 times before this crazy day.

I remember how it was an extremely hot summer day, and the older girl begged me to set up this thing called a "Slip and Slide"; it was this long, inflatable thing where the kids would go running toward it, slide across it, and then land in this tiny pool connected to the end of it. It had built-in sprinklers to make the toy even more fun and exciting.

Anyway, I was lying on the lounge chair, working on my tan while the kids ran all around, laughing and playing. My eyes were closed when the screaming started. At first, I didn't know that the screams were due to overwhelming pain; those girls were quite noisy as it was, so I assumed it was just all part of their fun and games.

"Vill, help!" the older girl yelled with desperation, demanding my attention. I then saw that the younger one running around the yard, her face furrowed and with tears streaming from her eyes. As I rushed over to her, it appeared as though she had a bunch of little spots all over her body. As I got closer to her, I realized that the spots were red ants. Those little bastards were so tiny, but they had somehow managed to swarm every inch of the child's skin, and it looked as though there were more of them by the second. Having no clue what to do and trying not to panic, I began swatting my hand at her skin. But it almost felt like it was no use; the more of them I removed, the more that seemed to appear. The child violently squirmed, making it incredibly difficult to remove the handful of ants that were dangling from her eyelids. Her sister did everything she could to help out. Finally, I commanded her to bring me the hose from the patio. I sprayed the child up and down with the cold water as she continued to scream and cry. I felt so bad for her.

The little girl screamed so loud and for so long that one of the nearest neighbors called the police. When they rushed into the backyard and saw the welts all over her body, they called for an ambulance. Fortunately, by that point, the cold water pressure had removed most of the tiny bugs; however, the paramedics were worried by the potentiality of a severe allergic reaction, so they loaded her into the ambulance and took her to the emergency room.

Of course, while I rode in the ambulance, I called her mother and father to tell them what happened. They were hysterical, and I was even worried that the mom was going to have a heart attack while she was on the phone with me. When I saw them at the hospital, the dad said something about how they had the grass treated so that the red ants wouldn't be able to build nests there, but then I guess he realized that too much time had passed since the last treatment. The grass was very soft and thick, so nobody had seen that the ants had built new nests. I would later come to learn that the backyard had many of them hidden in various places. So gross.

The older daughter said that her sister slid off the end of that the "Slip and Slide", and the bugs ran all over her immediately after; so, she accidentally slid onto a nest.

I was so relieved when I heard that the little girl didn't have a severe reaction to the ant venom, and the hospital allowed her to return home that same day. The doctor prescribed some strong anti-itch cream to the little girl because she said those bites could be some of the most annoying of all. And if you persist in scratching them, you prolong the time that it takes for your skin to heal. It seemed like she had hundreds, if not thousands, of those bite marks.

I was a bit worried that the parents weren't going to allow me to babysit anymore, but they didn't seem to blame me at all. I mean, how could they? I had never even heard of those aggressive ants before that horrifying day. Now I'm extremely careful whenever I walk in any grass in the state of Florida. Honestly, it's scary how many nests I spot regularly.

-Submitted by Vilena P.

Animal Attacks

Are you enjoying the read?

Due to the unexpected success of my books, I have decided to give back to the readers by making the following eBook **FREE**!

To claim your free eBook, head over to

www.LivingAmongBigfoot.com

and click the "FREE BOOK" tab!

Animal Attacks

Report #7

When I was ten years young, I went to stay at my Aunt's house in southern Wisconsin. She lived on a beautiful horse farm that was comprised of many, many acres. I thought it was the most magical of places; however, one day, that perspective would change.

It was Christmas Eve of 1996. My parents had dropped me off with my aunt and my older cousins because they invited me to stay at the farm a few days earlier. My aunt had recently acquired the place, so she was excited to have everyone within her extended family experience the wonderful environment. Seeing as how I was a pretty obnoxious little boy, I'm a bit surprised that they invited me.

Anyway, my aunt would host the Christmas Day celebration that year, so I had spent quite a bit of Christmas Eve getting everything organized for the event. It was in the evening when I was in the barn with my older cousin, John, helping him clean up the interior. It was while he was using a rake to organize some of the fallen hay that I decided it would be a good idea to walk around the horse and feed it a carrot. I have no idea what it was, but something startled the horse soon after I handed it the carrot. Out of nowhere, the magnificent animal rose onto two feet, and when it came back down, it sunk its teeth into my left shoulder and bit off a chunk. The force of the animal caused me to fall to the ground. I didn't even cry. I was in such an intense state of shock that it was as if crying was the last thing on my mind.

Cousin John rushed over to help me up; he then saw that there was a hole in my sweatshirt and that I was bleeding quite a bit. I remember him saying, "Holy shit!" right when he saw the wound. John is at least ten years older than me, so he was a lot more mature. He was able to stay composed through the whole situation, and he gave me a piggyback ride all the back to the main house.

It was the longest time before my aunt believed me that one of her horses

had bit me. I can't exactly blame her;
after all, that is extremely unusual
behavior for an herbivore—especially a
horse. Understandably, the employees of
the hospital were just as thrown aback
by my story. I remember my shoulder
was heavily bruised for quite a while, but
aside from that, everything healed up
pretty fast.

My intuition tells me that the
horse didn't mean to take a bite out of
me. I think it was very spooked by
something and failed to recognize that I
was standing underneath its head. I
think its mouth accidentally fell onto my
shoulder, and the weight of the animal
caused its teeth to dig into me. It's not as
if the animal consumed my flesh. Still, it
was a very traumatic experience for a
child, and it caused me to lose my trust
in horses. That would become an issue

later on in my life when I had a serious girlfriend who was obsessed with horse riding. No matter how many times I explained the frightening situation, she didn't seem to believe me. Her family had a horse ranch of their own, and they were always trying to convince me to ride with them. They would make fun of my story, and frankly, it caused a lot of tension between us. Of course, I might've downplayed the whole thing from the beginning, as I have been rather embarrassed by it.

That relationship didn't last, and it wasn't too long after the end, that I went to see a hypnotist, hoping that a few sessions with him would help me to conquer my fear. To my surprise, I did seem to make progress; however, I ended up falling off the horse the first time that I got back on one, and I was

forced to cope with a severe injury to my
ankle. The last thing I'll ever do is to go
near another horse.

-Submitted by anonymous

Report #8

I was only six years old when I had a horrible encounter with wildlife in my grandparents' backyard. It happened in an Illinois town known as Deerfield back in 1992. I spent a lot of time with my grandparents while growing up, and it was especially fun to go to their house in the summertime because they had a swimming pool in their backyard.

My grandma had a phobia of birds, no matter how small or harmless they seemed. It's really interesting when looking back at it because she was such a strong individual in every other way; truly, she was the bravest and most composed person I've ever known. I think I remember her mentioning an incident that happened to her when she was a small child, though I can't recall the details. I wonder if her phobia derived from PTSD.

In the gutter above the door that led to the backyard was a robin's nest. I believe there was a mama bird and three or four baby birds living in it. She was certainly protective of something up there because her head would perk up and she'd chirp like crazy whenever that back door opened and closed. My grandparents decided to leave the nest alone as a hopeful strategy that would help my grandma confront her demons. I remember it being there for a while without any issues, but then again, I think your perception of time is different when you're a child.

It was late morning when my grandma had just finished gardening and asked me to come out of the pool and head inside for some lunch. After I finished drying off, I helped her carry some of her gardening supplies inside. As I held the door open for her, that's when it happened. I heard her scream, and when I looked up, she was grabbing her forehead. It looked like she had just banged it against something.

"Grandma, are you okay?" I asked, very concerned because of how much I loved her.

"Something just..." she said, disoriented and in pain.

It was right as she moved her hand away from her forehead that the bird swooped down and jabbed at the left side of her head. She screamed and stumbled backward, losing her balance and falling onto her back.

"Grandma!" I yelled before rushing over to help her up. At first, I thought she was unconscious, but as I grabbed her hand and tugged, she used her other hand to push herself off the concrete. I was trying to rush her toward the door, but it was clear that her balance wasn't at its best. Again, she screamed, this time much louder than before, and I felt the weight of her body stumble away from me.

When I looked up at her face, I saw the angry mama bird violently pecking away; now, there was a lot of blood on her face. As my grandma swatted at the air, trying to smack the bird, she was unable to see where she was going. As she fell into the swimming pool, I could see her right eye was now mangled and protruding from the socket.

After she fell into the water, her body went limp. Knowing I wasn't yet strong enough to pull her out of the pool, I rushed inside to dial 911. Fortunately, my grandpa arrived home while I was on the phone and saw that I was crying. I dropped the phone and essentially pushed him out of the back door. Without hesitation, he jumped into the pool, fully clothed. The robin was still pecking away at my grandma's head, but my grandpa must've been able to deliver a smack that dissuaded it from returning. I vividly remember the sight of the water around my grandparents had taken on a red tint.

I did all I could to help pull my grandma out of the water, but I have to admit I was rendered nearly helpless by the vision of her eyeball hanging off of her face. Since I had dropped the phone while the emergency operator was still on the line, the police, paramedics, etc. came to the house and rushed her to the hospital. I was so afraid that she was going to die. I didn't know she had drowned or if she might bleed to death; I was young and had no idea how those kinds of things worked.

Luckily, my grandma survived. She did have to wear an eyepatch for the rest of her life, but aside from that, she made a full recovery. My grandpa took down that nest above the door as soon as we got home. I was scared that he was going to get attacked by the mama bird, but it seemed to have learned its lesson and never returned.

I always felt so bad for my grandma; she did her best to conquer her fear of birds and look where that got her. What's surprising was how she didn't allow that horrifying event to get the best of her; she continued to walk out into that backyard as if nothing ever happened. I remember asking her why she wasn't scared, and she would tell me how she was "too old to go through life being scared of silly things." When I look back at all of it, it was almost as if the trauma to her head transformed her perspective for the better. I imagine that most people would've been devastated by that level of attack and would've been too intimidated to be outside. My grandma was a real warrior, and I always think of her composure when I'm going through difficult situations in my adult life.

-Submitted by Devin M.

Report #9

Hello there, my name is Taylor, and my family and I faced a frightening encounter with a moose when we were on vacation in Yellowstone National Park back in 1991. My mom, dad, older sister, and I had been looking forward to the trip for a long time. Never in a million years did we think that we would undergo a near-death experience.

We had been in Yellowstone for almost a week, and I believe we were only one day away from departure when we decided to have a picnic in a random unoccupied field. We laid the blanket out on what I remember thinking was the greenest, lushest grass I had ever felt. I was 16 years old at the time, so I hadn't yet had a whole lot of experience traveling; the environment was so fresh and exciting to my senses. Everyone was having a great time, when all of a sudden, we heard a strange noise coming from the wooded area not too far from where we were sitting.

I think we were all worried that it was a large bear or something because none of us were educated enough to identify the noise. Nervously, we all stood up, carefully watching the area. Assuming we were about to head for our rental car, my mom began to pack things up. We all breathed a sigh of relief when the noise had stopped, and whatever was responsible had seemed to vacate the area.

It was soon after we had begun to settle that the large figure came bursting out of the forest. It was a large bull moose, and it was headed right for us. I remember entering a state of shock as I stared at the animal, amazed by how much larger it seemed than I had ever imagined. Due to my lack of movement, my dad yanked me up off the picnic blanket, forcing me to snap out of it and recognize that we were in extreme danger. Some of us veered off in different directions, which seemed to confuse the moose, and it slowed its charge right after it ran over our picnic blanket, crushing a few of the objects below. With little time to think, we ran in the direction of the car; thankfully, it wasn't too far off.

When I looked over my shoulder the first time, I could tell that the moose was still trying to decide who it should target. After we all dove into the rental vehicle, I looked out the window and was startled to see that the large mammal was well on its way toward us. Since it appeared to be headed toward my window on the rear left side, I quickly slid across the bench, smushing my sister against her window. She didn't even have time to push me away before we felt the impact of those massive antlers ramming against the car. Shards of glass burst onto the seat, and I could smell the animal as it violently shook the vehicle, tilting it off the ground.

Everyone screamed as my dad attempted to find the car keys; the impact had made him drop them right before he could insert them into the ignition. Luckily, he was able to grab them. He slammed on the horn while starting up the engine. It was clear that the angry moose did not appreciate the racquet, and it wasn't long before it backed away from the car. As we sped away, I could hear the loud grunts of the animal; it was pretty clear that it was warning us not to return. We were seriously lucky that the animal didn't damage the vehicle enough to the point where we wouldn't be able to drive it. Don't get me wrong; the vehicle was heavily damaged, but insurance companies are aware that things like that can happen, and they covered the costs.

I have to admit that that event prevented me from ever wanting to stroll around in areas of wilderness where large, aggressive mammals frequented. By no means are we the first family that had that kind of thing happen to them; I suppose that's just the risk you take by journeying through our beautiful national forests.

-Submitted by Taylor B.

Report #10

My ex-husband and I faced a frightening ordeal while we were on a camping trip on the big island of Hawaii. The attack was so abrupt, and I'm so grateful we were able to survive it.

We had had a very active day, so both of us were able to fall asleep quickly that night. I remember I was having the most relaxing rest when, all of a sudden, it felt like a bulldozer had rammed straight into our tent, instantly knocking the wind out of me, as I was the one nearest to that side of the tent.

"Holy shit!" I yelled out, stunned by both the pain and surprise. My ex-husband struggled to burst out of his sleeping bag and grab the flashlight. I could hear the snorts as I scrambled to stand up and find the tent's exit. The last thing I wanted to do at that moment was to go outside, but it seemed that being stuck inside the tent was a surefire path toward further injury.

After I undid the zipper and was pushing my way out of the tent, I was instantly taken off my feet by the force of the stinky creature. After it knocked me to the ground, it went toward my ex-husband and bit onto his leg while he was fumbling to put his pants on.

"Get off of me!" he screamed, trying to shake his leg from the animal's clutches. I got up and ran over to the dark figure and started pounding my fists across its back, desperate to get it off of my ex. Eventually, it released him but then quickly turned around and clamped its jaws onto my ankle. I could hear more pigs snorting somewhere in the vicinity as I tried to yank at my attacker's ears and scrape at its eyes. I could see that the animal wasn't of extraordinary size, but it felt as if it was of extraordinary strength.

As I continued clawing at the pig, I was nearly blinded by the flashlight as my ex powered it on before using it to bash the creature's skull. I guess the wild animal had had enough after three or four clunks on its noggin, and it dashed out of the tent. Wanting to ensure that it didn't return, my ex ran after it, aggressively hollering.

"What're you doing!?" I yelled, worried that he was going to be attacked by the pack of pigs or whatever you call it. "Come back!"

The volume of the squeals seemed to skyrocket as my ex must've gotten extremely close. I was so worried that I was going to hear him scream from being attacked by multiple pigs at once, but it wasn't long before the racquet began to quiet.

I didn't even want to look down at my bare leg; I could tell it was bleeding heavily. When my ex hobbled back to the tent, I could see the skin around his lower leg was ravaged. Fortunately, we had a first aid kit with us, so we used alcohol to clean the wounds, all while nervous that the pigs might return. After using a few shirts to compress our wounds, we drove to the nearest emergency room. This event happened about seven years ago, so we were able to use GPS to find a place. That's something I often ponder—I don't know what we would've done if we hadn't had smartphones to guide us to a medical center. It's scary to think that we might've lost too much blood if we had to drive around aimlessly. I remember I felt rather faint as we pulled into the facility's parking lot.

We ended up making a full recovery, but that event gave us the scare of a lifetime. Neither of us had any idea that feral pigs could be that aggressive. We went to Hawaii knowing that the islands lack natural predators, so perhaps that notion caused us to drop our guards entirely. Now, whenever someone tells me that they're going to

Hawaii, I make sure to warn them about those wild pigs. And if that one pig was able to cause that much harm to us, imagine what it could do to a child or a small pet. I strongly feel as though it's a danger that should be talked about more often.

-Submitted by Stephanie F.

Report #11

For the first 42 years of my life, I had never had a confrontation with an animal. That's probably partially because I had only lived in Minnesota; however, I'd come to learn that if you're not careful, midwestern wildlife can be extremely dangerous. The following recount happened in the summer of 2015.

People call me Bucky. My wife and I still live in the same house where the encounter took place. We live on a typical suburban street—one where people frequently walk their dogs and wave to one another. It's probably one of the least threatening environments that one could ever come across.

For whatever reason, our garbage seemed to be singled out by the raccoons. Every once in awhile, they'd go for the trash of others, but it was usually our containers that would end up spilled all over our driveway and the connecting street. I never figured out why they were so attracted to our trash. It was always such a mess that the trash collectors were unable to do anything with it. Additionally, it had started to happen so regularly, that it was making our front yard look like a garbage dump. There were even a few times where neighbors walked or drove by while giving me judgmental, condescending looks. Sure, that might've been in my head, but the reality was that both my wife, Rosalyn, and I, were very embarrassed by the constant mess. We take pride in keeping things tidy.

We had tried an array of strategies to deter the coons from our property, but none of them seemed to hold up. We even called animal control on multiple occasions, but the critters would always flee as soon as the vehicle turned into our driveway. This issue started taking up loads of our time since we had become so fixated on getting rid of them.

There was this one night where I had had a few too many drinks, following a lousy day at work, when I heard the familiar noise of the trashcans tipping over and spilling the contents across our driveway. The timing of it pushed me over the edge; I grabbed a broom and ran out the front door, ready to swing. Most of the raccoons fled, but it was as soon as I hit one of them with a broom that another one emerged from the spilled trash can and leaped onto my chest. I immediately felt the sharp claws penetrate the fabric of my shirt, and then my skin. I couldn't believe how heavy the animal felt as it landed on me; I had always thought of them as being comparable to the weight of a plush toy. It felt as though a medium-sized dog was scratching and biting at me.

The aggression caught me off guard completely, which caused me to trip and fall onto my back on my driveway. As I tried to rip the critter away from me, it had bitten into the skin below my chin. I couldn't help but scream out from the pain. Luckily, one of my neighbors happened to be driving by at that moment and glimpsed the mayhem. He immediately parked the car and ran over to help me. It only took one solid kick to the animal's gut, and it was launched off of me. I didn't see it, but my neighbor said that the raccoon landed on its feet and started dashing back toward us, hissing like a monster.

It was right before it returned to us that it suddenly did a 180 and bolted up the sidewalk and then around one of the neighbor's alleyways, disappearing from our line of sight.

As my neighbor, Eric, helped me off the ground, his eyes looked wider than ever; it was like he had seen a ghost. I then felt the sensation of liquid dribbling down my torso and realized that blood was squirting from the underside of my jaw, all over my clothes and my driveway. When Eric guided me inside, my wife began screaming. She would tell me later that it looked to her like someone had used a knife to slash at my throat. She called 911 and got an ambulance to rush me to the hospital.

When I arrived in the ER, one of the first things they did was administer a rabies shot. For those of you who don't know, they put the needle in your stomach; it's rather uncomfortable. I'd come to learn that the animal was indeed infected with rabies, which was what prompted it to be so aggressive.

It's safe to say I'll never approach raccoons the same way, and if you ever have a similar problem with the animals constantly spilling your garbage, I highly recommend you refrain from getting too close. I consider myself lucky to have survived.

-Submitted by Jerry B.

Report #12

Hello, my name is Kyle, and I had an unfortunate experience when I came home from college to visit my family in Waco, Texas. This will probably sound weird, but I once had a pet duck. His name was Don (short for Donald) and I loved that animal with all my heart. He traveled with me nearly everywhere, as long as I didn't have to get on an airplane.

I acquired Don from a farmer who I used to work for on the weekends while I was in college. He had only recently reached adulthood, and I guess it was because I used to feed the ducks bits of bread that one of them started following me around more than the others. That particular duck was Don. He'd often keep me company while I was completing tasks around the grounds, and I quickly noticed that he didn't make much noise; for whatever reason, the animal rarely quacked.

There was this one time where I was leaving work, and Don hopped into the car through the window. My boss saw the whole thing and laughingly suggested I take the duck home for the night, just to see what happens. My roommate, Tarik, instantly gravitated toward Don, and our apartment quickly gained fame amongst our campus. Random students would sometimes drop by to meet Don, even attractive girls. In a way, it was like Don had become the school mascot, even though our true mascot was anything but duck-like. It was quite interesting how much good energy he seemed to bring to the area.

When I brought Don home to see my family in Waco, my Mom and two sisters were thrilled; my younger sister, Hannah, couldn't stop laughing at how much personality he had. She loved how he followed me around the house, seemingly always open to discovering new places.

It was particularly warm that summer, so my mom, out of the goodness of her heart, purchased one of those inflatable kiddie pools from the local grocery store. We set it up in the backyard, and Don immediately took to it. We had been out there for an hour or so, and I was watching Hannah toss breadcrumbs into the pool when we suddenly heard loud barking coming from the neighbor's property. I barely had time to react before the stalky Dobermann pinscher came leaping over the wooden fence that divided the properties and ran straight for the kiddie pool.

It seemed like neither Hannah nor I had the chance to react before the large dog snatched Don in its jaws and sprinted over to another section of our yard. As I ran toward the dog to save my pet, it looked as though there was a hailstorm of feathers while the dog savagely shook Don in its mouth. I tackled the Dobermann hard enough to where Don was able to waddle a few steps away. It was as I watched my pet collapse that I felt the canines pierce the skin on my forearm. As Hannah ran and picked Don up off the grass, I yelled at her to run inside. While I tried to fight off the vicious dog, I heard an awful snapping sensation, and I immediately knew that it was one of the bones in my right arm. The force of the dog was so immense that it felt almost impossible to shove it off of me.

Fortunately, the sound of its owner whistling caused the dog to release its grasp, and it went running back toward the section of the fence that it had jumped over. It must've been the dog's first time visiting our property because it looked puzzled as to how it was supposed to return home. I had to notify the neighbor, Rich, that his dog was over at our place. When I met him around the side of our house so he could walk in and get his dog, he didn't even seem concerned by the amount of blood that was dripping from my arm. If anything, the look in his eyes implied that it would be bad news for my family if we reported his dog to the authorities. Because of that, I wasn't quite sure how I should proceed.

I could hear the sound of my mom and sisters crying as I entered the house through the backdoor. They were all standing around Don's lifeless body. They had known him for such a short time, but they quickly learned to love him. After I went to the hospital for treatment, we had a beautiful burial for the beloved duck.

It turned out that my sister told the authorities about Rich's dog, and when they approached him, he punched one of the officers in the face and ended up getting arrested on multiple charges (I'm not exactly sure what for, aside from an assault on an officer). Nobody knows what happened to the neighbor or his dog, but my family never saw him again.

-Submitted by Kyle G.

Are you interested in Tom's experience with the sasquatch species?

The popular "Living Among Bigfoot" series is now available on Amazon, Audible, and iTunes!

Animal Attacks

Editor's Note

Before you go, I'd very much like to say "thank you" for purchasing this book.

I'm aware you had an endless variety of books to choose from, but you took a chance on my content. Therefore, thanks for reading this one and sticking with it to the last page.

At this point, I'd like to ask you for a *tiny* favor; it would mean the world to me if you could leave a review on this book's Amazon.com page.

Your feedback will aid me as I continue to create products that you, as well as others, can enjoy.

Animal Attacks

Newsletter Signup Form

Don't forget to sign up for the newsletter email list. I promise this will not be used to spam you, but only to ensure that you will always receive the first word on any new releases, discounts, or giveaways! All you need to do is visit the following URL and enter your email address.

URL-

https://mailchi.mp/f70052976ad4/whenanimalsbite

Animal Attacks

Social Media

Feel free to follow/reach out to me with any questions or concerns on Instagram. I will do my best to follow back and respond to all comments.

Instagram:

@living_among_bigfoot

Animal Attacks

About the Editor

With music as his primary passion, Lars Ryan moved to Nashville, Tennessee to pursue his dream of earning a living via the strings of his acoustic guitar. While constantly writing songs, it dawned on him that he might also enjoy the art of writing books, but he never knew what to write. Eventually, Lars would undergo a terrifying encounter with a large cat and would later use the experience to propel his interest in writing.

You can email him directly at:

when.animals.bite@gmail.com

Printed in Great Britain
by Amazon

19884763R00068